CARMEN OUT TO PLAY!

A collection of children's playground games

Compiled by Heather Russell

Illustrated by Peter Viska

Melbourne
Oxford University Press

ACKNOWLEDGEMENTS

Some of the games in this book came from the Australian Children's Folklore Collection, which is housed at the Melbourne University Archives. Some of them came from my own and other adults' memories of childhood games, and some were taught to me by the children who attended Debney Meadows Primary School, Flemington in 1984–85. Thanks to all those children for their enthusiasm and willingness to teach me their games. Thanks also to Peter Leman, June Factor and Gwenda Davey for their encouragement and advice.

OXFORD UNIVERSITY PRESS

Oxford New York Toronto
Delhi Bombay Calcutta Madras Karachi
Kuala Lumpur Singapore Hong Kong Tokyo
Nairobi Dar es Salaam Cape Town
Melbourne Auckland
and associated companies in
Berlin Ibadan

OXFORD is a trademark of Oxford University Press.

© Text Heather Russell 1989
© Illustrations Peter Viska 1989
First published 1989

National Library of Australia
Cataloguing-in-Publication data:

Russell, Heather.
   Carmen out to play!

   ISBN 0 19 554918 X.

   1. Games — Australia — Juvenile literature.
   2. Play — Australia — Juvenile literature.
   I. Viska, Peter. II. Title.

796.1'0994

Typeset by Bookset, Melbourne
Printed in Australia
Published by Oxford University Press, 253 Normanby Road,
South Melbourne, Australia

INTRODUCTION

The games in this book are special for two reasons: firstly, children usually learn them from each other and not from adults, and secondly, the rules of these games are never fixed — you can always change them to suit you and your friends (as long as everyone in the game agrees).

Many games in this book were taught to me by children in the playground, so I decided to put some of those children in this book so they could teach *you* how to play.

In this book you'll meet four children — characters you'd find in any Australian playground. I've nicknamed them **Gooseneck** and **Pepper** (they're the girls) and **Stickynose** and **Spike** (they're the boys), and they will show you how to play the games.

When you're reading this book remember that Gooseneck, Pepper, Stickynose and Spike will show you only *one* version of each of the games — there are actually lots of different ways of playing.

If you know different versions of these games, I would be very happy to hear about them. I would also like to hear about other games that you play with your friends in the playground, backyard or wherever! You can write to me at the address below.

Heather Russell

Heather Russell
Australian Children's Folklore Collection
The Australian Centre
University of Melbourne
Parkville   Victoria   3052

CONTENTS

CAN'T CATCH ME, YOU DIRTY OLD FLEA!
CHASEY GAMES   7

BAGS NOT HOLD THE END!
SKIPPY GAMES   23

HOP, HOP, HOP TO THE LOLLIPOP SHOP!
HOPSCOTCH GAMES   35

COPY CAT FROM BALLARAT!
PENCIL AND PAPER GAMES   49

SPIKE

Favourite Games: Gang Tiggy, Five Stones.
Hates playing: Jocks, Fortune Telling

BRAIN
Full of ideas for new games and new rules.

HANDS
Like a sieve, always dropping things, especially jacks.

MOUTH
Always open, always talking always organising always teasing his friends.

POCKETS
Overflowing with stones, bits of string, taws and sticks.

SHORTS
Worn in any weather. (hot or cold)

KNEES
Scabby, from home base dives.

LEGS
Muxly, solid, good for sprinting.

MARBLES

V.

2

STICKYNOSE

Favourite Games: Jacks, Hang the Butcher
Hates playing: Skippy

NOSE
Always poking itself into other people's business.

HANDS
Big. Perfect for playing jacks.

EXPERT TEASER
Especially when playing Hang the Butcher. Classic insults like 'When God was giving out brains, you thought he said milk shakes so you asked for a THICK one.'

EARS
Hear more than they should.

BRAIN
Sharp, overloaded with jokes, smart remarks, stupid riddles and funny rhymes. Run when you hear KNOCK KNOCK...or... Did you hear the one about...or... Fat and Skinny... or...Why did the chicken...

POCKETS
Always bulging with jacks, pencils, paper, books and fortune tellers.

V.

3

GOOSENECK

Favourite Games: Hopscotch, Fly, Cat & Mouse
Hates playing: Skippy

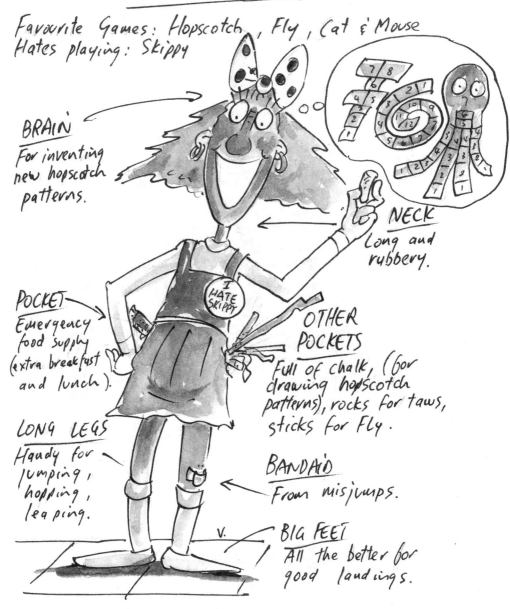

BRAIN
For inventing new hopscotch patterns.

NECK
Long and rubbery.

POCKET
Emergency food supply (extra breakfast and lunch).

OTHER POCKETS
Full of chalk, (for drawing hopscotch patterns), rocks for taws, sticks for Fly.

LONG LEGS
Handy for jumping, hopping, leaping.

BANDAID
From misjumps.

BIG FEET
All the better for good landings.

PEPPER

Favourite Games: Skippy; Hello, Hello, Hello Sir.
Hates playing: Chasey

BRAIN
Chock-a-block full of rhymes like:
Teddy Bear, Teddy ... or
Cowboy Jill ... or
Roses are Red... or
Over the Garden wall ... or
Spike, Spike come to tea... or
Strawberry Shortcake,
Blueberry Pie.

HAIR
Always very
neat

MOUTH
Like a
megaphone —
Everyone can hear
her skippy rhymes,
especially 'UP THE
MURRUMBIDGEE.'

ROPES
Best collection
of skipping ropes
in the school.
Long, short,
thick, thin.

**FUMBLE
FINGERS**

POCKET
Stuffed with old
stockings for Hello,
Hello, Hello, Sir.

LEGS
Short but strong
and muscley: good
for jumping but
useless for running.

v.

CAN'T CATCH ME, YOU DIRTY OLD FLEA!

CHASEY GAMES

CHASEY: MARKING OUT THE BOUNDARIES

Before playing games of Chasey or Tiggy, it's important that all the players decide where the boundaries of the game will be. Everyone must know which territory is out of bounds and which territory is 'in'. Remember, if you go out of bounds, you are 'it'.

If the area you choose for your Chasey game is too big, then it will be very hard for the person who is 'it' to tig anybody. Chasey is usually more fun if you mark out a small area.

HIDE AND SEEK

Before you start, decide on the boundaries of the game. Hide and Seek needs an area with plenty of hiding places, and a clearly marked 'home base'.

To start the game, find out who will be 'it'*. Try this rhyme:

> One potato, two potato, three potato, four,
> Five potato, six potato, seven potato, more.
> Bad spuds, you're out!

*How do you work out who will be 'it'? See page 106.

Gooseneck is 'it', so she closes her eyes and counts to 20 while all the other players run away and hide.

Now Gooseneck has to find everyone, and tig each player before they get back 'home'. The ones who get 'home' without being tigged are 'safe'. If you are tigged, you team up with Gooseneck and help her to find and tig the others.

10

TRAIN TIGGY

Play Train Tiggy somewhere in the playground where there are lots of lines marked out on the ground.

No one is allowed to run off the lines. If you do you are 'it', and if you're tigged you are 'it'.

*'Barley' means time out for a rest.

KING

(also known as Ball Tiggy or Brandy)

Before you start, decide on the boundaries of the game.

To start, find out who will be 'it' in this special way:

Stand in a circle and bounce the ball into the middle of the circle. Everyone tries to kick the ball out of the circle through someone else's feet.

If it goes out of the circle through a gap *between two people's feet*, shout 'broken window' and start again.

When the ball is kicked out of the circle through *one person's feet*, then that person is 'it'.

Now we know who is 'it' the game is simple. Pepper chases the others with the ball. If the ball hits you, you're 'it'.

FIVE STONES

Five stones is a Chasey game played in two teams: a fielding team (this team does the chasing) and a bowling team. (This team is chased by the others.)

Before starting:

1 Decide on your boundaries. Five Stones needs a fairly big area because there are lots of players.

2 Decide on captains for each team. The captains toss a coin to see which team will 'bowl' first.

The bowling team starts the game by setting up a pile of five stones. Using a tennis ball, the bowling team takes turns to try and knock over the pile of stones. The fielding team stands by and watches.

As soon as the stones are knocked over, the bowlers all disappear, and one of the fielders grabs the ball.

The fielders have to get each member of the bowling team out by hitting them with the ball. Meanwhile members of the bowling team sneak up to the stones, and try to build up a pile again without getting hit.

The game is over when the five stones are all piled up again (which means that the bowling team wins), or when all the bowlers have gone out (which means that the fielding team wins). At the end of a game, the two teams swap sides, and you start the game again.

I'M OUT-CH!!

GANG TIGGY

Before starting, decide on your boundaries. Try a small area for Gang Tiggy, e.g. half a basketball court.

To start, try this rhyme:

>Tic tac toe
>Here I go
>Where I'll land
>I do not know.

The last person left in the circle is 'it'.

As soon as Stickynose realizes he is 'it', he starts to chase everyone. If he tigs you, you're 'it'.

But if you think you are about to be tigged and you can't get away, you can say 'gang', stand like this, and then you're 'safe'.

You only say 'gang' when you have to, because being 'gang' means you can't move. But, if another player touches you, you're free to run around again. If everyone is 'gang' at the same time, then the first one who said 'gang' is 'it'.

Remember, if you are tigged, you are 'it'.

CAT AND MOUSE

Let's say Gooseneck is 'it', so she's the mouse. She runs around the circle and taps each person on the head as she goes, saying: 'Mouse, mouse, mouse, mouse, mouse, mouse, mouse, *cat*'. She chooses Stickynose to be the Cat.

Stickynose has to jump up, chase Gooseneck around the circle, and try to beat her back to his place.

He doesn't beat her, so he's the next mouse. But, if he had arrived back at his place *before* Gooseneck, then *she* would have been the mouse again.

BAGS NOT HOLD THE END!

SKIPPY GAMES

PLAYING SKIPPY

A game of Skippy needs about three metres of rope. You can buy all kinds of different rope at hardware shops.

Skipping rhymes make the game much easier. If the rope turners and the skippers all chant the rhymes together, then the skippers know when to skip, and the rope turners know how fast to turn the rope.

Each skipping game in this section has its own special rhyme. Learn each rhyme by heart before you start playing. The words or syllables (parts of words) written in bold type **like this**, should be chanted a bit louder than the rest of the rhyme because the skipper must skip on these particular words.

Before starting a game, you must work out who will hold the ends of the rope. Try this rhyme:

> Mickey Mouse had a house
> What number was it?

The person who is tapped on 'it' says a number — let's say three. Three is spelt out around the circle. The person who gets the last letter 'E' is out. The rhyme is repeated over and over until there are only two people left in the circle — they hold the ends.

COWBOY JILL

This is Pepper's favourite.

Skip through the whole rhyme, doing the actions.
On the word 'go', you run out, and the next person
runs in.

UP THE MURRUMBIDGEE

Up the Murrum**bidg**ee
If you **miss** a loop you're **out**!

Each person skips once, then runs out of the rope as the next person runs in — without missing a loop.

Keep chanting the rhyme over and over, so that everyone is running through the rope, keeping in time with the rhyme. If you muck up the rope, or miss a loop, then you take the end.

ROSES ARE RED

Let's say Pepper starts skipping. At the end of the
rhyme, she names a friend who runs into the rope
and skips with her.

The two friends chant the rhyme again, then on the
last line, Spike calls a friend in.

Soon everyone is skipping.

GRANDPA, GRANDPA

Let's say Spike starts. He skips through the rhyme, then on the last word, 'in', the rope-turners do 'pepper'* until he mucks it up. Everyone counts his 'pepper' skips. Now it's the next person's turn and Spike takes the end.

*'Pepper' (also known as 'hot') means that the rope is turned as fast as possible.

31

JANUARY, FEBRUARY . . .

As players chant the months of the year, each skipper does one skip, then runs out (the same as in Up the Murrumbidgee). The skipper who lands on December stays in the rope while the rope turners do 'pepper'. This time it's Gooseneck, so she has to skip as fast as possible until she mucks up the rope. Everyone counts how many 'pepper' skips she does.

Try this variation: the skipper who lands on his or her birthday month has to do 'pepper'.

HOP, HOP, HOP TO THE LOLLIPOP SHOP!

HOPSCOTCH GAMES

HOPSCOTCH

Before you start, find a taw. Gooseneck uses a flat rock which is not too small and not too bouncy.

To decide who will go first, throw your taw over your shoulder. The player whose taw lands closest to (or in) Square 8, starts the game.

Throw your taw into Square 1, then hop through the Hopscotch pattern.

36

If you get through without making a mistake, throw
your taw into Square 2, and hop up and down the
pattern the same way as before. Keep going up to
Square 8.

RULES FOR HOPSCOTCH

1 Never step on a line.

2 Never hop into a square that has a taw in it.

3 Decide before the game starts, whether you are allowed to balance yourself by putting one hand or two hands on the ground — or none at all.

4 If you throw your taw into a square and it lands on a line, then it's a 'liner', and you have another go. If it lands outside the square you're aiming for, it's the next person's turn.

If you break any of the above rules, it's the next player's turn. Your taw stays in the square you were on, ready for your next turn.

CLAIMING A 'HOUSE'

Once you've reached Square 8, you can keep the game going and make it harder by claiming a 'house'. Stand at the top of the Hopscotch pattern with your back turned and throw your taw over your shoulder. The square that it lands in is your 'house'. Put your initials in it. This is now your rest base and nobody is allowed to hop in it except you. Now put your taw in Square 1, and start from the beginning again.

PARTNER'S HOPSCOTCH

Hold hands with your partner and jump through the
hopscotch pattern as usual. The rules are the same as
those described on page 36, but the two players must
never let go hands. If one player makes a mistake,
then both are out, and it's the next couple's turn.

How can Pepper and Spike turn around at the top
without letting go of each other's hands?

COLOURS HOPSCOTCH

This is quite a different Hopscotch game. You need two players. Let's say Gooseneck's the caller and Stickynose is the hopper. Draw this pattern on the ground.

P = Purple   I = Indigo
R = Red   M = Mauve
G = Green   Y = Yellow
B = Blue   O = Orange

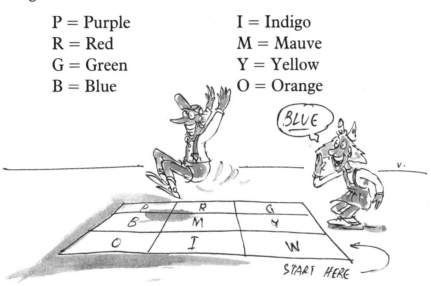

Stickynose has to hop to each different square, depending on the colour Gooseneck calls. The first time around, Stickynose has to hop on his right foot. If he steps on a line, or if he hops into the wrong square, he's out, and it's Gooseneck's turn to hop.

41

When he has hopped into each square, he hops into
the 'Start here' square and begins again. But this
time he has to hop on his left foot.

The third time through he has to hop with his legs
criss-crossed.

The fourth time he has to do it all with his eyes shut.

FLY

Before starting, collect ten sticks from the playground. Place them on the ground at least 15 cm apart (a bit less than the length of your foot).

Players line up behind the sticks. The first player in line is called the SPIDER. Last in line is called the FLY.

Each player steps between each of the ten sticks.

If you touch a stick you're out.

When it's the Fly's turn, she does the same as everyone else.

But at the last stick, she takes as small, or as big a jump forward as she feels like.

She lands.

Then she turns around and chooses one stick from
the row of ten.

The Spider picks up the stick and puts it on the spot where the Fly landed.

Now you start all over again. Everyone steps or jumps through the row of sticks in the same order as before.

When the Fly has her next turn she jumps, lands, and chooses another stick which is placed at her feet.

Gradually the sticks get spread further and further apart. More and more players go out.

The last person left in plays the Fly in the next game.

If the Fly goes out you can either choose a new Fly from those players still in the game, or start a new game with a different Fly.

COPY CAT FROM BALLARAT!

PENCIL & PAPER GAMES

S-O-S

S-O-S is like a huge game of noughts and crosses. You can play it on any size grid. Before starting, draw up a grid like this:

RULES FOR S-O-S

1 Each player can write either 'S' or 'O' in a square.

2 If you make an 'S-O-S', then you score one point and have another turn.

3 The player with the highest score wins.

HANG THE BUTCHER

This is a game for two people: a hangman and a butcher.

The hangman chooses a word, and the butcher has to try and guess it — letter by letter.

Let's say Stickynose is the hangman and Pepper is the butcher.

Here's how you draw a hanging tree.

If the letter that Pepper guesses is in Stickynose's word, then Pepper writes 'E' (for example) in the correct space.

If the letter she guesses is not in Stickynose's word, then he's allowed to draw one stroke of the 'hanging tree'.

Hang the Butcher is a race to see whether Pepper can guess Stickynose's word before he finishes drawing the 'hanging tree'.

52

FORTUNE TELLER

(also known as Chip Chops and Saltcellar)

A Fortune Teller is a device for tricking people,
insulting your friends, telling their future, and
sending secret messages. It is made of paper folded
in a particular way so that the messages,
compliments or insults are hidden in the folds.
Friends (or enemies) have to answer a series of
questions before they get one of the messages.

Make a Fortune Teller with page 55. Follow instructions on page 57.

You may write any message you like: insults, compliments or predictions for the future. Some examples:

'You're beautiful.'

'You look like a pig.'

'You will marry a rich pop star.'

Make up four different messages for your Fortune Teller.

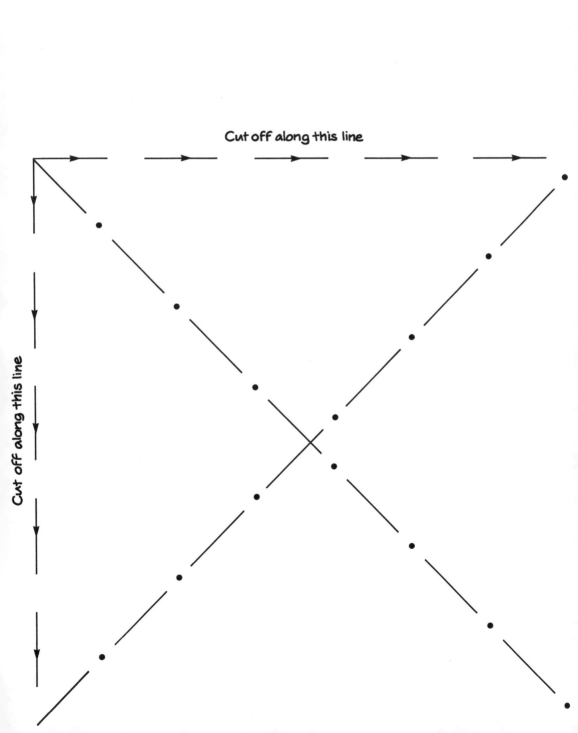

Cut off along this line

Cut off along this line

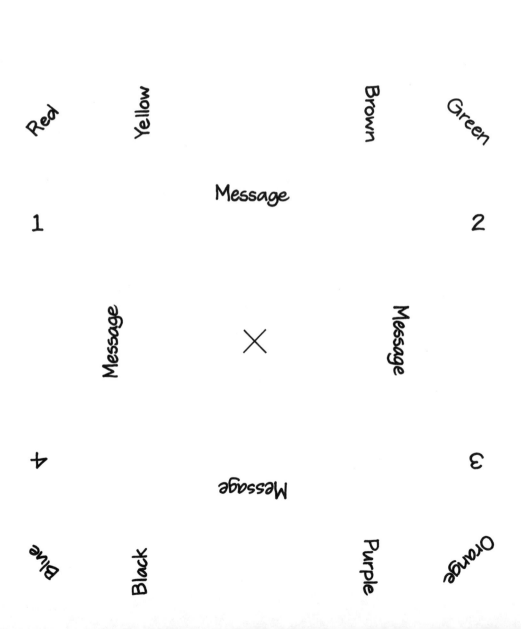

Red

Yellow

Brown

Green

Message

1

2

Message

✕

Message

4

3

Message

Blue

Black

Purple

Orange

INSTRUCTIONS FOR MAKING A FORTUNE TELLER

Step 1 Cut the paper on page 55 along the lines marked:

———▶——   ———▶——   ———▶——

Now you have a square piece of paper.

Step 2 Fold paper along the lines marked:

———— • ———— • ————

Leave the paper folded out.

Step 3 Fold each of the four corners into the centre point of the square. Leave your Fortune Teller folded over like this:

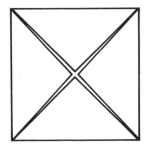

Step 4 Turn your Fortune Teller over to the other side. Fold each of the four corners into the centre, marked: ✕

Step 5 Fold your Fortune Teller in half so it looks like this:

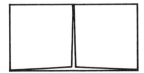

57

Step 6 Fold it in half again so it is a very small
square.

Step 7 Let your Fortune Teller unfold to look like
this:

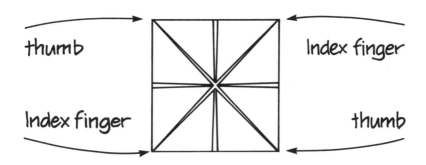

Place your two thumbs and index fingers in
the flaps underneath each corner.

Step 8 Your Fortune Teller is now complete. Open
and close it by alternately pressing together
your two thumbs and two index fingers and
the thumb and index fingers of each hand.

HOW TO PLAY WITH A FORTUNE TELLER

Remember, you may write any kind of message —
insults, compliments or a 'fortune' underneath the
flaps as indicated on page 56.

SURPRISE! SURPRISE!

GAMES OF SURPRISE

MOTHER MAY I?

Before starting, choose a home base where 'Mother' stands. All the other players stand along the starting line about ten metres away.

PLAY ← ABOUT 10 PACES →

To start the game, find out who will be 'Mother'.
Try this rhyme:

Ooza Tooza
Vocka Tooza
Vee, Vi, Vo,
Vanish!

Mother tells each player in turn to move a certain number of steps towards home base. She also tells them what type of steps to take. For example, she could say: 'Gooseneck, take six jumps', or, 'Stickynose, take three ant steps', or, 'Spike, take seven ballerina steps'.

Other types of steps you can take are hops, leaps, twirls, crocodile steps etc. Make up your own!

Stickynose, Spike and Gooseneck must always obey Mother's instructions. Before moving, each must say, 'Mother may I?'

If you forget to say 'Mother may I?', you have to go back to the starting line. The first person to reach home base is the next Mother, and the game starts again.

PUSS IN THE CORNER

Before starting, find an area where there are four corners (say, in the shelter shed), four pillars (under the school perhaps), four poles, or four dustbins.

To start the game, here's a quick way of working out who will be 'it'.

LAST ONE TO THE SHELTER SHED IS 'IT'!

Each player has a pole or a corner except Gooseneck who is 'it', and stands in the middle. Players swap poles whenever they want to. Gooseneck has to try and grab a pole when the others change over. After a changeover, the person left without a pole is always 'it'.

QUEENIE, QUEENIE

To play Queenie, you need either a tennis ball or a
basketball. The person who owns the ball usually
starts off Queenie.

8
BIG
STEPS

Queenie stands about eight or ten big steps away
with her back to the other players. She throws the
ball over her shoulder.

Someone catches it and hides it. Queenie must not
look around until she hears the chant:

Queenie, Queenie, who's got the ball?
Is she big or is she small?
Is she fat or is she thin?
Or is she like a rolling pin?

When the chant is over, Queenie turns around and tries to guess who is hiding the ball. She is only allowed three guesses.

If Queenie doesn't find the ball in three guesses, then Stickynose, who was hiding the ball, is the next Queenie. If she does find the ball, then she has another turn as Queenie.

STATUES

Before starting, decide on a home base and a starting line (about fifteen big steps away). Find some 'treasure' (such as a rock, or a stick, or a ball), and place it at home base.

To start the game, find out who will be the keeper of the 'treasure'. Try this rhyme:

> Little Miss Pink fell down the sink.
> How many miles did she fall?
> Close your eyes and think.
> One, two, three . . .

Players line up along the starting line. Stickynose, who's the 'keeper', stands with his back to them. Players sneak up on Stickynose while his back is turned. As soon as he turns around everyone freezes. If he sees a player moving, he sends them back to the starting line.

Pepper reaches the treasure first, so she grabs it, and tries to get back to the starting line without being tigged. If she does, she's the next 'keeper'. If Stickynose tigs her, then he's the 'keeper' again.

70

FUMBLE FINGERS!

BALL GAMES

GAMES WITH JACKS

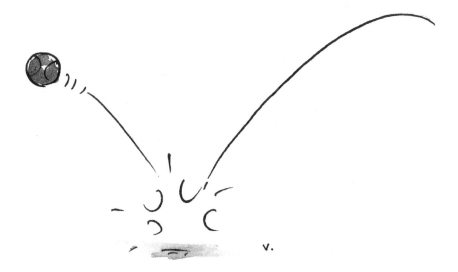

HELLO, HELLO, HELLO, SIR

This is a game you usually play by yourself.

Before starting, find an old pair of pantyhose and cut off one of the legs at the top. Find a tennis ball, put it right down into the foot of the pantyhose, and tie a knot to keep it fixed in place.

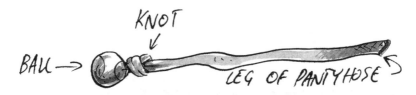

Stand with your back against a wall. Chant the following rhyme in time with the ball as it bounces against the wall on either side of you. Each time the word 'Sir' comes up in the rhyme, you must bounce the ball under your raised left leg.

Here's the rhyme:

> Hello, hello, hello, Sir.
> Going to the show, Sir?
> No, Sir. Why, Sir?
> Because I've got a cold, Sir.
> Where'd you get the cold, Sir?
> At the North Pole, Sir.
> What were you doing there, Sir?
> Catching polar bears, Sir.
> How many did you catch, Sir?
> One, Sir. Two, Sir, Three, Sir. Four, Sir. Five, Sir.
> Six, Sir. Seven, Sir. Eight, Sir. Nine, Sir. Ten, Sir.
> All the rest were dead, Sir.

Remember, always *start* with the ball on your *right* side.

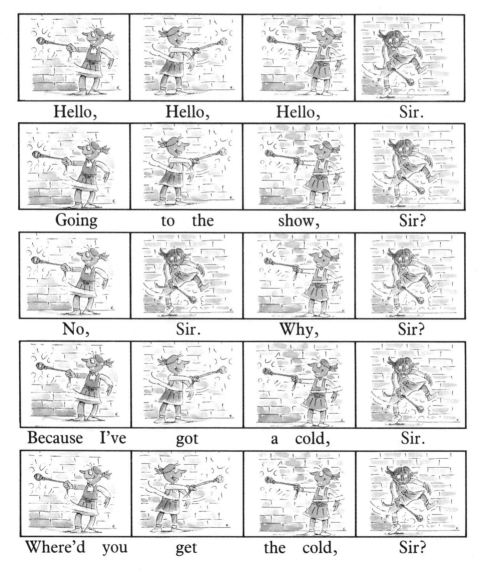

Hello,	Hello,	Hello,	Sir.
Going	to the	show,	Sir?
No,	Sir.	Why,	Sir?
Because I've	got	a cold,	Sir.
Where'd you	get	the cold,	Sir?

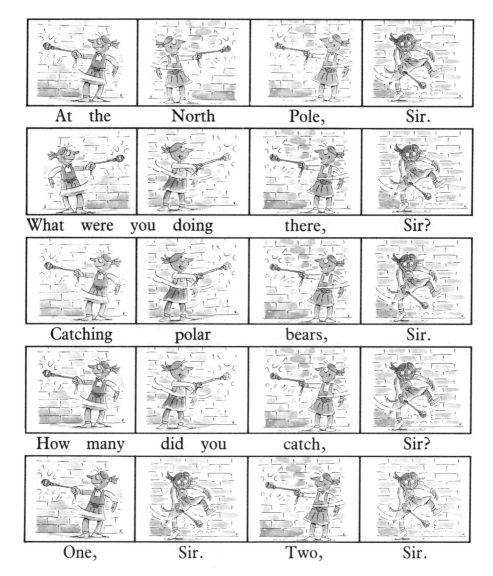

At the North Pole, Sir.

What were you doing there, Sir?

Catching polar bears, Sir.

How many did you catch, Sir?

One, Sir. Two, Sir.

Three, Sir.   Four, Sir.

Five, Sir.   Six, Sir.

Seven, Sir.   Eight, Sir.

Nine, Sir.   Ten, Sir.

All the rest were dead, Sir.

SEVENS

This is another ball game you play up against a wall.
You can play it alone, or with friends. In Sevens
there are seven different actions. You have to
complete each action properly, and do it the correct
number of times (without dropping the ball), before
going on to the next one.

Here are the seven different actions:

Sevens Throw the ball
against the wall and catch it on
the full. Do this seven
times in a row.

Sixs Throw the ball so it hits
the ground, then the wall.
Then, catch it on the full.
Do this six times.

Fives Pat bounce the ball on the ground five times.

Fours Throw the ball under your raised leg. Catch it on the full as it bounces off the wall. Do this four times.

Threes Throw the ball against the wall, and as it comes back, pat bounce it three times. Do this three times.

Twos   Throw the ball against the wall. Clap your hands in front, behind, then in front of you again. Catch the ball on the full. Do this twice.

Ones   Throw the ball against the wall, turn around on the spot, and catch the ball on the full as it bounces off the wall. Do this once.

RULES FOR SEVENS

1 Always start at *Sevens* because that's the easiest action, and work through to *Ones*, which is the hardest.

2 If you drop the ball, or don't do the action correctly, then it's the next person's turn. When it's your turn again, you start with the action that you mucked up last time.

3 After *Ones*, you go back to the beginning again, but this time you must stand on the one spot — you can't move around to catch the ball.

4 The third time through it's harder again. You have to catch the ball using only one hand.

5 Harder still, try throwing and catching the ball with your opposite hand. (If you're right-handed, use your left hand and vice versa.)

DONKEY (I)

Any number of friends can play this game. The
person with the ball starts. (A basketball or soccer
ball is the best sort of ball to use in this game.)

Spike's got the ball, so he goes first. He throws it
against the wall, then he jumps over it as it bounces
back off the wall. The ball has to bounce between
your legs without touching you anywhere. After
you've had your turn, you go to the back of the line.

If the ball hits you, or if it doesn't bounce between your legs, then you're 'D'.

If this happens again, you're 'D-O'. The third time, you're 'D-O-N' and so on. When you get to 'D-O-N-K-E-Y', you're out of the game.

Hint for Donkeys

Throw the ball carefully. Run to the spot where you think it will bounce, and jump right over this spot, just as the ball is hitting the ground.

DONKEY (2)

Donkey is an easy game to start — the person with the ball throws it up in the air and starts the game by yelling out one player's name.

All the other players scatter.

Gooseneck grabs the ball and yells *freeze*. Everyone stands still.

Gooseneck chooses a target and takes three giant steps towards him.

She has to try and hit her target on the leg. The target mustn't move his feet, but he can move anything else.

She hits him, so now Stickynose is 'D'. He immediately starts the game off again by throwing the ball up in the air, and yelling out another name.

RULES FOR DONKEY (2)

1 If you throw the ball at your target and *miss*, then *you* are 'D'. And, if your target catches the ball on the full, then *you* are 'D'.

2 Let's say your name is called and you catch the ball as it comes down (on the full). You must immediately throw the ball in the air again, and yell out someone else's name. No one gets a 'D' when this happens.

3 If you make six mistakes, you're D-O-N-K-E-Y, and out of the game.

GAMES WITH JACKS

Before playing, you must have a set of five jacks (or knucklebones, as they used to be called). You can buy plastic ones either from a supermarket or a toy shop, or get knucklebones (free) from some butcher shops. Knucklebones from a leg of lamb are bigger, heavier, and much easier to play with than the plastic jacks from a toy shop.

If you collect five 'real' knucklebones from a friendly butcher, ask an adult to boil them on the stove for five or ten minutes so they are clean and ready to play with. Try painting them different colours, or boiling them with food dyes so that you have your own special set.

There are two basic procedures or skills that you must learn before you can play a game of Jacks. The first one is called Overhands.

HOW TO DO OVERHANDS

Throw the five jacks in the air and catch as many as
possible on the back of your hand.

Throw up the jacks on the back of your hand, and
catch as many as possible in the palm of your hand.

You must also learn how to pick up a jack.

HOW TO PICK UP A JACK

Choose a taw. Throw your taw in the air.

While your taw is still in the air, pick up one jack off the floor. Catch your falling taw.

Now you are ready to play a game of Jacks.

88

PLAINS

Ones

Step 1 Do Overhands. (See page 87 for instructions.)

Step 2 Put aside the jacks that you caught in Overhands. Choose a taw from the jacks that you dropped.

Step 3 Pick up the remaining jacks one by one. (See page 86 for instructions.)

Twos

Do steps 1 and 2 as in *Ones*.

Step 3 Pick up the remaining jacks two at a time.

Threes

Do steps 1 and 2 as in *Ones*.

Step 3 Pick up the remaining jacks three at a time. (Don't worry if there are less than three jacks — just pick up as many jacks as there are left.)

Fours

Do steps 1 and 2 as in *Ones*.

Step 3 Pick up the remaining jacks four at a time (or, pick up the jacks that are left).

RULES FOR PLAINS

If you make a mistake, or drop a jack, it's the next person's turn. On your next turn, start at the same place where you made the mistake.

SCATTERS

In Scatters you do not do Overhands.

Scatter Ones

Scatter the five jacks across the floor. Choose one for your taw. Pick up the other four jacks one at a time.

Scatter Twos

Scatter the jacks and choose one for your taw.

Pick up the jacks two at a time.

Scatter Threes

Scatter the jacks and choose one for your taw.

Pick up three jacks in one go, then the last jack by itself.

Scatter Fours

Scatter the jacks and choose one for your taw.

Pick up all four jacks together.

92

RULES FOR SCATTERS

If you make a mistake, or drop a jack, it's the next person's turn.

Once they are scattered, you must not touch, knock or move any jacks other than the ones you want to pick up. You must pick up the jacks from where they are scattered.

NO FENUDGE!

GAMES WITH MARBLES

FIRING OR FLICKING MARBLES

How you fire or flick a marble depends a lot on where you were born, your age, and the school you go to. Here are some different ways of flicking that you may not have seen before:

Marbles come in all colours, sizes and patterns and can be bought fairly cheaply from toy shops and supermarkets. Galaxy, ghosty, bird cage, spaghetti, beachbum, oily, hot rod, bloodsucker, cat's eye — these are just a few names made up by children to describe the different types of marbles that you can collect. You can build up a collection of marbles by swapping, winning, finding, buying or even inheriting some from parents, grandparents (or other adults who used to be Marbles fanatics).

RULES FOR MARBLES

There are a few basic rules that apply to all games of Marbles, and these rules should be agreed on *before* the game begins.

1 *'For keeps' or 'for friendlies'*

'For keeps' means that you get to keep the marbles you win off your opponents. 'For friendlies' (or 'no keeps') means you give *back* the marbles you win.

2 *'No fenudge'*

'No fenudge' means no cribbing your hand forward before firing your marble. If you're caught 'fenudging', the penalty is usually losing a turn.

3 *'Clears' or 'no clears'*

'Clears' means that you can clear away any sticks, stones or other obstacles between you and your target. (By the way, Marbles is best played on bare dirt rather than concrete or grass.) If you can't move the obstacle, you can move your marble in an arc to get around it. 'No clears' means you can't do this.

FOLLOWS

This game is usually played by two people. Each player needs only one marble. To decide who will start, draw a line on the ground. Each player tries to throw his or her marble as close to the line as possible.

Spike is closest so he starts. Spike fires his marble away. Stickynose then fires his marble towards Spike's and tries to hit it. To win the game you have to hit your opponent's marble three times in a row.

Spike and Stickynose take it in turns trying to hit each other's marble.

Bull's eye! Spike now gets another shot. He hits it, but then he misses on the third shot. Now it's Stickynose's turn again. If he hits Spike's marble three times in a row, then he's the winner and he gets to keep the marble (if the game is 'for keeps').

IN THE RING

Scratch out a circle in the dirt. If you're just learning how to play, make it quite small, but if you're good at Marbles, make the circle as big as you like.

SCRATCH OUT THE CIRCLE WITH A STICK, SHOE HEEL OR A BARE BIG TOE!

ABOUT 30CMS

ABOUT 1 METRE

Any number of players can play this game, usually up to four or five is best. Each player puts in the same number of marbles — let's say three or four marbles each. Put in the most common ones such as cat's eyes — don't put in your favourites!

To decide who will fire first, each player throws a marble towards the edge of the circle.

The player closest to the circle (but not in the circle) goes first, the second closest goes second etc.

Spike wins the throw in so he fires first. He fires his taw (his favourite firing marble) from the edge of the ring and tries to knock as many marbles as possible out of the ring. Any marbles you knock out belong to you.

RULES FOR IN THE RING

If you miss, or don't hit a marble out of the ring, it's the next person's turn.

If you hit a marble out of the ring, and your taw goes out too, then you keep the marble but you don't get another turn.

If you hit a marble out of the ring and your taw stays in the ring, then you have another turn.

At the end of your turn, pick up your taw and keep it until your turn comes around.

Always fire your taw from the edge of the ring.

Decide before you start a game whether it will be 'for keeps' or not.

HOLES

Scratch out four holes in the ground to make your own Marbles course. It's a bit like a golf course — once you've got the hang of the game, you can vary the course to suit yourself. To decide who will start off the game, each player stands on the starting line and throws a marble towards the fourth hole.

Gooseneck gets nearest to the hole, so she starts. She fires her taw (her favourite shooting marble) from where it landed in the throw in, towards the first hole. Her taw misses the hole, so she leaves it where it lands, and Spike has his turn.

The aim of the game is to get your marble into each hole. The winner is the first one to get right around the course to the fourth hole.

RULES FOR HOLES

When your taw lands in a hole, you get another shot.

If someone else's marble is in your way (or even if it's not in your way, but you feel a bit cheeky), you can try to hit it off course.

WHO IS 'IT'?

Most of the games in this book are group games which need a special person to get the game started, e.g. someone to be 'it', or someone to be the 'Mother' in Mother May I?, or two people to hold the ends of the rope for Skippy.

There are many different ways of working this out, but one very popular way is to tap out a rhyme on everyone's feet. Let's use the rhyme:

> Tic tac toe
> Here we go.
> Where I'll land
> I do not know.

Each player puts one foot in the middle of the circle. One person chants the rhyme, and for each word of the rhyme he or she taps one player after another on the foot. The person who is tapped on the *last* word of the rhyme goes out of the circle, then the same process is repeated again. At the end of the rhyme, another person is eliminated.

The rhyme is repeated over and over until only one person is left. That person is 'it'.

There are hundreds of different rhymes you can use. You'll find more in this book, and in collections of rhymes and chants such as *Far Out, Brussel Sprout!*, *All Right, Vegemite!*, and *Unreal, Banana Peel!* all compiled by June Factor and published by Oxford University Press.

FINALLY . . .

The games in this book can be played anywhere — at school, in the playground, in the street, in your backyard, on the beach, in the living room — any space you can find.

Wherever you play them, it's up to you to adapt the rules to suit the place where you are playing, how many people you are playing with, and how good you are at the game.